The Ultimate Blueprint To Create Wealth and attain financial freedom:

How to generate and maintain long lasting wealth using basic principles

By

Michael J. Bowman

TABLE OF CONTENTS

Introduction

Wealth is commonly thought of in terms of money and material goods, but it can also apply to other forms of assets such as property and investments. Achieving a level of wealth can bring a sense of security and freedom, allowing for financial independence and the opportunity to fulfill our objectives and aspirations.

Wealth creation is vital for everybody and everyone since typical savings plans may not always be enough to complete major obligations.

The possession of a strong source of income is not always enough to protect your economic future and for that reason, you also have to acquire an investment portfolio that will provide long-term income from several sources.

The process of building wealth emphasizes how to invest your money in a way that will create an income-generating asset. As a result, wealth is not defined as per your income level.

Having riches doesn't just give you money to buy items; it offers you freedom and control over your life.

The most practical strategy to build money as an employee or a business owner is to use your financial savings as a foundation to build and protect your wealth on. The revenues earned by your investment portfolio will allow you the ability to maintain a high level of life that satisfies your present and future wants and desires.

As a business and financial coach, I have met different people from many spheres of life, and in as much as these people are talented in their specific fields, they generally lacked an in-depth and broad understanding of the field of financial investments which is a major problem that this book aims to solve.

Chapter One

Generating and building wealth

The practice of creating long-term revenue from a variety of sources is known as wealth creation. This extends beyond income derived from work and comprises savings, investments, and any other assets that generate income. It also depends on sound financial planning and understanding of one's long-term financial objectives. Building wealth over time from nothing is inevitable by simply following basic steps and sticking to them. These steps include:

1. Learn about money

Generally, before we can really tackle any more significant changes in all spheres of our lives, we first need to make changes to our attitude (mindset).

"Anyone can create a financial ark to endure and thrive in the future," stated business tycoon and Rich Dad, Poor Dad author Robert Kiyosaki. "However, in order to construct an ark with a strong foundation, you must devote time to your financial education."

Hence, devoting time to your financial education is the first step towards creating riches out of nothing. Acquaint yourself with key phrases like earnings, costs, net worth, investment return, passive income, and financial independence, to name a few. Take classes, read books, listen to interviews and podcasts, and read blogs like Sarwa's that provide financial knowledge. Remember that, similar to all forms of education, financial education needs to be an ongoing endeavor. Never give up learning. Make sure you only follow respectable blogs that will point you in the direction of resources from dependable and prosperous business owners, investors, and financial experts.

2.Make sure you acquire a consistent source of income and make enough money to meet your basic necessities and save some extra.

You must begin earning money as soon as possible. Although it might seem simple, this is the most important stage for individuals who are just getting started. Earned income and passive income are the two main streams of income generation. While passive income is obtained via investments, earned money is the result of your work. You might not have any passive income until you have saved up enough cash to begin investing.

Without a steady stream of income, it is difficult to create riches from nothing. Without saving money, you cannot invest, and without a steady source of income, you cannot save.

This means that multilevel marketing, Ponzi schemes, or gambling do not help people create lasting wealth.

Acknowledge and disregard those who tout easy ways to get rich fast, like working three hours a week to accumulate wealth. The source of sustainable wealth is long-term value creation. You can't really generate sustainable wealth if you're not producing goods or services with intrinsic worth and making money from them. Thus, if you don't already have a job, find one now, and if you do, hold onto it.

As a small business owner, keep your attention on adding greater value over the long run. According to self-development guru Brian Tracy, "all wealth comes from adding value," which involves creating a company plan that can "produce more, better, cheaper, faster, and easier than someone else."

Investing in your education and skill set is a smart strategy to increase your income potential. Acquiring advanced academic degrees, certifications relevant to your sector, and training courses are all helpful in developing your human capital.

3.The next line of action is to control your expenditures in order to optimize your savings.

This can be achieved through tracking your expenditure, making and adhering to a budget, and cutting back on needless or pointless spending. Making and following a budget is essential if you want to learn how to create riches out of nothing.

Using the previously mentioned regular source of income, you must now establish a monthly budget in order to get control over your expenditures. A budget is a financial plan that includes projected income and expenses for a given time period.

It is necessary for every household and/or person to establish a monthly budget in order to determine their anticipated income and estimated expenses. Living without a set budget is like trying to navigate the financial world without a map, and you can be sure that you'll end up lost in the mists of money.

A well-liked method for budgeting is the 50:30:20 rule. Using this method, you can create a budget that allocates 50% of your income to necessities (such as rent, mortgage, food, and medical costs), 30% to luxuries (such as entertainment, travel, and shopping), and 20% to savings and investments.

Generally speaking, you should set

aside 50% of your income for fixed expenses (such as rent, utilities, insurance, etc.), 20% for savings and investments, and 30% for variable costs (like entertainment, travel, food, etc.). You can, however, modify these percentages based on your objectives and unique circumstances.

Budgeting is crucial because it makes it simpler to find areas where you can make savings and investments by letting you know how you spend your money. You may save and invest more money if you spend less.

By developing your skill set, you may also manage and grow your money.

If you work, enhance your skill set by

enrolling in specialized courses and devoting yourself to ongoing professional growth. Enhancing your hard and soft talents will help you acquire better job offers from other firms or promotions, which will increase your salary.

If you run a small business, you should give your clients greater value, devote more resources to innovation, and deepen your grasp of the market. You can raise your revenue and market share by doing this.

Investigate options for passive income as well. Apart from augmenting your earnings from your occupation or enterprise, you ought to investigate diverse prospects for generating passive revenue.

In contrast to your job or business, passive income is the money you make that doesn't need your constant presence or labor.

For those of us studying how to create riches out of nothing, passive income is essential. Remarkable investor and CEO of Berkshire Hattaway Warren Buffett once stated, "You will work until you die if you don't find a way to make money while you sleep."

Investment passive income, in which your money does all the work, and non-investment passive income, in which you perform some side labor, are the two categories of passive income. We'll go with the latter for the time being because the former is the subject of the following section.

There are lots of options to make extra money in the modern global and digital economy. However, be cautious of schemes that promise rapid riches, such as Ponzi schemes and online betting, when investigating these prospects.

Among the dependable and tested suggestions for passive income are, but are not restricted to:

• **Selling digital items**

If you are an authority in a certain

field, produce books, paid webinars, video courses, email courses, or other digital products on subjects that people find interesting. Digital items have the benefit of just requiring one creation (apart from potential upgrades). You may make money off of just one product for a very long period.

• Blogging

You can market your idea through a run of consistent blog entries as an alternative to selling it as a digital product. Your blog can be made profitable by a variety of methods, including Google Adsense, digital goods, paid memberships, sponsorships, and guest posts after it receives a certain amount of traffic.

• Affiliate marketing

You can sell other merchants' products on your site and get paid a commission for each sale, as an alternative to selling your own digital goods. You can stop making your own products by using affiliate marketing.

• Drop shipping

This method allows you to sell other merchants' products without having to stock them yourself. Orders are placed by customers with you, who then forward them to the producer for delivery to the customer. Your income is the difference between the purchase price, which you pay to the merchant, and the retail price, which the client pays.

4.Take a pass on active investment.

To ensure that your money is appropriately diversified throughout time, the final stage is to invest it in a range of various assets. Investing can help you reach your financial objectives, keep ahead of inflation, increase your money over time, and create passive income. But, there are hazards associated with investing, so before you begin, you should be aware of your time horizon, your risk tolerance, and your investing goals. Additionally, you must investigate the many investing options—stocks, bonds, mutual funds, exchange-traded funds (ETFs), real estate, etc. and select the ones that best fit your requirements and tastes.

You must first invest your money in order to accumulate it. If you have done the aforementioned actions, you are currently saving at least 20% of your take-home pay and generating additional cash from other side projects. It's time to put the two together and get serious about investing. Every single one of the millionaires you know and respect gained their wealth through prudent and successful stock market investments. You will have to perform the work if you are not paid to do it. The issue is that contrary to Buffett's advice, you cannot make money while you sleep and your earning potential is restricted. However, when you invest your money in the market, it works for you and you get to benefit from other people's labor.

What are the best investment opportunities to build wealth from nothing?

1. Stock ETFs

Investing in company shares is a highly effective means of accumulating money. You gain from the company's increasing worth as a shareholder since it works for you.

The exchange-traded fund (ETF) market is the best place to purchase stocks. ETFs are passive funds that are more affordable, transparent, low-risk, and have longer-term profitability.

Investing in exchange-traded funds (ETFs) allows you to diversify your holdings without the costs, taxes, and market timing associated with buying individual equities, which entails significant risk.

You can diversify your equity holdings by using stock exchange-traded funds (ETFs). ETFs for stocks that track developed economies, emerging markets, and the US are available for purchase. You can also diversify based on industry (financial, technology, etc.) and market cap (big, medium, and small).

Stocks offer the highest returns on investing even if they carry greater risk than other asset classes. A solid diversification plan will help you reduce risk and increase returns.

2. Bond ETFs

Governments and businesses use bonds, which are debt instruments, to raise capital. Federal bonds are issued by the federal government, municipal bonds are issued by government bodies, and corporate bonds are issued by businesses. They repay the money they borrow from you with interest.

The best way to purchase bonds is through ETFs, just like stocks.

Compared to stocks, bonds are less riskier but give lesser profits. On the other hand, they lower the portfolio's total risk when paired with stocks.

3. REIT ETFs

Instead of renting or buying and selling real estate properties, which is very risky, REITs (real estate investment trusts) provide an alternative way to profit from the real estate industry.

REITs are equities of real estate firms that buy and sell real estate as well as mortgage companies that offer consumers with financing and mortgage companies that provide the finance to customers.

When the value of the real estate or mortgage company rises, your money grows in value; those companies are working for you. REITs pay a very high dividend (they are mandated to pay at least 90% of income as dividends), which provides extra investable income for you.

ETFs are the greatest way to purchase REITs, much like stocks and bonds.

.

Chapter Two

The Psychology of an Investor

A careful balance between risk and reward, analysis and intuition, characterizes investing as both an art and a science. Investing is essentially about allocating resources with the intention of producing lucrative returns over an extended period of time. Investors often have a lot of questions about business concepts. Ultimately, the primary goal of an investor is to assess a company's future and determine whether more investment is warranted. Investors are interested in learning whether a business idea has the potential to succeed, is practical, and can be turned into a profitable endeavor.

The qualities of a successful Investor are as follows. They are as follows:

- **Be patient**

An astute investor recognizes that success is a gradual process. They are prepared to stick with their investments despite market swings in order to avoid making snap decisions based on transient volatility. They can profit from the compounding effect over time if they are patient.

- **Order (Discipline)**

It is imperative to establish and adhere to a well-defined investment strategy. Sense-driven investors avoid the need to follow trends or hop on trains. They avoid emotional biases impairing their judgment by using a systematic strategy to influence their decisions.

- **Capabilities for Analysis**

Strong analytical skills are possessed by successful investors. They carry out in-depth investigations, closely examining economic statistics, market movements, and financial statements. They are able to make wise financial decisions because of their analytical skills. This analytical prowess enables them to make informed investment choices.

- **Managing Risks**

Effective risk management is what makes good investors different from complete risk avoidance. They spread out their holdings over several businesses, asset types, and geographical areas. Effective risk management is what makes good investors different from complete risk avoidance. They diversify their portfolios across different asset classes, industries, and geographies. This strategy exposes investors to possible high-growth prospects while assisting in mitigating losses during recessions.

- **Continuous Learning**

The investment landscape is ever-evolving. Proficient investors possess a strong desire to learn and are dedicated to remaining current with market trends, technology breakthroughs, and financial advances.

The Attitude of Investors

★ **Long-Term Vision**

A savvy investor stays away from the

minutiae of the here and now and instead concentrates on the wider picture. They are aware that market swings are only momentary and that their investments will eventually pay off in full.

★ Emotional Intelligence

Choosing investments based solely on feelings can backfire. Sensible investors strive to separate their emotions from their decisions and are conscious of their emotional biases. Because of this, they are able to make logical choices even when the market is turbulent.

★ Humility

Astute investors recognize that they

are not the only ones with the solutions. They are willing to receive professional advice, grow from their mistakes, and modify their tactics as necessary.

★ Flexibility

As the world of investing is ever-changing, wise investors are flexible. Companies are able to adjust their tactics in response to macroeconomic fluctuations, technical advancements, and shifting market conditions.

The following advice will assist you in cultivating an investor's mindset.

- **Create a plan of action.**

Although it's simple to convince oneself

to start investing, it makes little sense to do so in the absence of a clear plan of action. Learning as much as you can about the specific market you are interested in should be your initial move. Do you wish to make FX investments? If so, set aside sufficient time to get proficient in the fundamentals and educate yourself on the various approaches to avoid squandering your hard-earned cash.

- **Foster a drive for achievement.**

Have you ever noticed how you drag yourself to work but then get really excited to work on your side project when you get home? Most of the time, desire is the main factor influencing how passionate you are about various activities. If you're driven enough to achieve, you can create a clear route in the direction of generating riches.

- **Seek assistance from those in your vicinity**.

There are trainers, coaches, and consultants working with employees or even top executives of huge corporations in almost every area you can think of. Asking for help from others doesn't always have to be seen negatively. It might be exactly what you need to learn more from people with greater experience in your specific industry. Setting reasonable objectives and making baby steps toward them is much easier when you have a mentor to aid you along the way.

• Acknowledge defeat (losses)

Throughout their lives, even the wealthiest investors have suffered significant losses. But their recognition that losses are a part of the financial game is what makes them unique. It's just not possible to succeed every single time. However, you are more likely to make wise selections that increase the likelihood that your money will increase if you take the time to conduct your study.

• Take action now

It's possible that procrastination is the

only thing holding you back from beginning your investing career. If you are constantly coming up with excuses, nothing will ever be done. You'd best stop blaming others and start blaming yourself if you've told yourself over and over that "interest rates keep going up," "I don't have the time to learn about financial markets," or "I should have bought this stock five years ago." Those who choose not to act make these justifications. It's time to break this bad habit and begin setting aside time on a weekly basis for your investing efforts. Investing should no longer be considered a side pastime; it should be treated like a business. Even if you read every piece of advice from wealthy investors, nothing will change unless you take these actions yourself.

Chapter Three

The concept behind investing in Stocks and Bonds.

An equity, or stock, is a security that indicates ownership of a percentage of the issuing firm. The term "shares" refers to units of stock that provide the owner a share in the company's assets and earnings in proportion to the number of shares they possess. Stocks are the cornerstone of many individual investors' portfolios and are mostly bought and sold on stock exchanges. Government rules designed to shield investors from dishonest business practices must be followed while trading stocks.

Stocks offer investors the greatest opportunity for growth, or capital appreciation, over an extended period of time. Long-term stock investors—say, those who have stuck with the market for 15 years or more—have typically seen robust, positive returns. Investing in stocks is a good idea because they make it simple to create a diversified portfolio that spans numerous industries. By doing so, you can lower your total risk profile and increase profits on your investment portfolio, which may also include bonds, real estate, and cryptocurrencies.

Investors buy bonds as a dependable source of income. Bonds usually pay interest on a fixed timetable, like every six months. Bonds are a means to protect capital when investing, as bondholders receive their entire principal back if the bonds are held to maturity.

With bonds, you purchase an investment whereby you consent to lend money to a business or government for a predetermined period of time at a predetermined interest rate. In exchange, you receive interest payments from the government or firm for a predetermined period of time, on top of the bond's initial face value.

A bond's face value Is the amount you will receive back when the bond matures, and its coupon amount is the annual interest paid.

Purchasing bonds via a broker, mutual fund, exchange-traded fund, or straight from the government is the most popular method.

★By Means Of A Broker

Similar to buying stocks and other investments, you can purchase bonds through a broker. Investors are usually the ones selling the bonds you purchase. You could be able to purchase the bond for less, depending on the state of the interest rate market.

★By means of the Government

Direct purchase of government bonds is available from the government.

Since stocks and bonds are easier to manage and invest in than derivative instruments like futures and options, they are among the most popular investments made by novice investors. It is advised to allocate approximately one-third of one's income to stocks and bonds.

Chapter Four

Investing in real estate and commodities

When looking for places to invest your money, there are a lot of options. Stocks, bonds, mutual funds, exchange-traded funds, and real estate are all wise investment choices regardless of your level of experience; forex and cryptocurrencies can be too volatile for beginners. A profitable and fulfilling investing approach is purchasing and holding real estate. Unlike stock and bond investors, prospective real estate owners may use leverage to buy a property by paying a portion of the whole cost up front and then paying back the remaining amount over time, plus interest.

Why is investing in real estate a wise decision?

A prudent investment is likely to result in a profit. A high potential benefit should be included in an investment that carries a high degree of risk in order to balance it out. But even if you choose assets with a high chance of success, it's not a certainty. You should avoid making any financial ventures, including real estate investments, if you cannot afford to lose the money.

These are the top five methods for real estate investors to profit.

- **Rental Establishments**

Owning rental properties may be a great choice if you have the time and skills necessary to handle tenants and renovations. There are viable opportunities both within the state and outside of it with local properties.

- **Real Estate Investment Groups (REIGs)**

For those who wish to own a rental property but don't want to deal with the management duties, REIGs are a great option. Investing in Real Estate Investment Trusts (REITs) requires having a cash cushion and financing available.

- **Buying and Selling Homes**

House flipping should be pursued by someone with significant experience in real estate appraisal, marketing, and renovating. Flipping houses demand money and the capacity to monitor or perform necessary renovations.

- **Investment Trusts for Real Estate (REITs)**

A real estate investment trust (REIT) is the ideal choice for investors who want portfolio exposure to real estate without engaging in a typical real estate transaction.

- **Internet-Based Real Estate Portals**

There are real estate investing platforms for those who would like to pool their funds with others to take part in larger commercial or residential purchases. The investment is made through online real estate platforms, sometimes known as real estate crowdfunding. This requires less capital than buying a piece of real estate outright, but it is still required.

The best real estate crowdfunding

platforms give investors the ability to combine their funds with those of other investors looking to lend money to start-up or continuing real estate projects, giving you the opportunity to diversify your holdings with little initial outlay of funds.

Raw resources or agricultural goods that are exchangeable on the market are known as commodities. Global events and trends, together with supply and demand, all have an impact on them. They are a cheap starting cost and short-term investment, but they come with a lot of risk, volatility, and fees. Nonetheless, investors may benefit from commodities' growth potential, inflation protection, and portfolio balance.

★ Options

These are agreements that grant you the right, but not the responsibility, to purchase or sell a good at a certain price and time in the future. With this technique, you can speculate on market swings on hedge your position with minimal risk. But it also entails problems with liquidity, temporal decay, and premiums.

★ Exchange-traded funds (ETFs)

These are investment vehicles that mimic the movements of a commodity index or a basket of commodities. By using this strategy, you can enter the commodity market with minimal fees and maximum liquidity while diversifying your portfolio. But it also includes market risks, management costs, and tracking failures.

Putting one-third of your income toward buying commodities and real estate is crucial.

Chapter Five

Investing in liquid assets

An asset that is easily convertible into cash or cash on hand is referred to as a liquid asset. Because it can be sold cheaply and with little effect on its value, an asset that is easily convertible to cash is analogous to cash itself. A liquid asset is the most basic type of asset. Both corporations and consumers use them. A liquid asset is something that can be quickly changed into cash or is readily available as cash.

Since liquid assets don't lose value when they're sold, they are thought to be almost equivalent to cash.

An investment having a short maturity period, including stocks, bonds, and mutual funds, that may be swiftly converted to cash is called a cash equivalent.

Non-liquid assets, like real estate, cars, or jewels, can be more difficult to sell and turn into cash quickly than liquid assets. It's possible that they won't get their full price.

An asset cannot be deemed liquid until a number of conditions are met. The product needs to be in a well-established market with lots of potential customers. It must be simple to transfer ownership.

Liquid assets often carry lower risk than nonliquid assets. If you have at least some liquid assets in your portfolio, you can always access a certain level of cash value, even in the event that nonliquid asset values decline significantly due to market fluctuations.

The fact that liquid assets have your cash on hand whenever you need it is their greatest advantage. Emergencies occur without warning. Investors are frequently recommended to keep some assets in their portfolio in order to easily access their funds in the event of an unanticipated emergency. Keeping liquid assets in your portfolio, such as money market funds, is quite advantageous.

These resources not only preserve your funds for unexpected expenses but they can also be used to make additional investments. You are free to use your assets whenever you choose to make new investments without having to sell any of your current holdings.

These assets also have the benefit of being relatively less hazardous than non-liquid assets. These assets can be quickly and fully sold when the market is in a panic. A consistent income stream can be obtained by investors from certain liquid assets, such as dividend-paying equities and fixed-income exchange-traded funds (ETFs).

Generally speaking, it's also a good idea to allocate one-third of your income to buying liquid assets.

Chapter Six

The concept behind risk management during investing

In the language of finance, risk is the possibility that the actual returns on an investment or outcome will be different from the projected or expected returns. Risk entails the potential to lose all of your initial investment.

The potential to lose everything of an investment is a component of risk.

Identification, analysis, acceptance, or mitigation of uncertainty in investment decisions are all part of risk management. To put it simply, it's the process of keeping an eye on and managing the financial risks involved with investing. In essence, risk management is the process by which a fund manager or investor assesses and attempts to quantify the possibility of losses from an investment, such as a moral hazard, and then decides what course of action—or course of inaction—to follow in order to achieve their goals and tolerance for risk.

The process of Identifying, analyzing, accepting, or mitigating uncertainty in investment decisions is known as risk management. It is the procedure for locating, evaluating, and ranking any risks, and then putting plans in place to lessen or mitigate their effects. By taking a proactive stance, companies may safeguard their resources, good name, and long-term prosperity.

In the world of investments, risk and return are inextricably linked.

Avoidance, retention, sharing, transferring, loss prevention, and minimization are some of the risk management techniques.

Standard deviation, a statistical measure of dispersion around a central tendency, is one strategy used to determine risk. The main goals of risk management are to recognize and evaluate any risks, create plans to reduce or eliminate them, and keep an eye on and evaluate how well these plans are working.

By assisting in the calculation of uncertainties and the prediction of their effects, risk management provides companies with a foundation upon which to make decisions. By responding proactively rather than reactively, it mitigates or minimizes the implications of risk even before it occurs, thereby preparing the company for the unexpected.

You can anticipate the following advantages of financial risk management:

- **Determines the risk exposure**

The identification of an organization's risk exposure is the first step in the risk management process, according to risk management certification programs. The main method used by an organization to address the risks found in the finance function is its financial risk management function.

The measurement and classification of

the financial risks to which the organization is exposed, as well as the measurement and classification of the risks to which it is not now exposed, are the main duties of the financial risk management function.

Maximizing the return on an organization's financial assets while lowering asset risk is the main objective of the financial risk management function.

- **Calculates the risk exposure in numbers**

Calculating the risks to the company in monetary terms is another main objective of financial risk management, according to courses on the subject. In order for the management to prioritize them while addressing them.

The finance department needs to apply quantitative and qualitative risk-assessment methods and techniques in a systematic, methodical manner in order to accomplish risk management objectives.

In-depth knowledge of risk measurement, responsible risk-management guidelines, and risk-control procedures are additional prerequisites. Analysts quantify a financial risk in numerical figures using a variety of techniques and tools, such as standard deviation.

There are methods available for

standard deviation that help analysts measure how much risk an organization is exposed to in terms of potential financial threats. For example, small businesses frequently utilize Excel as software for financial analysis.

- **Promotes risk reduction**

Once you have the risk estimates, you need to take appropriate and timely action. At this crucial point, the most vital considerations are: Can your company afford to take the risk? And how could it be mitigated the best if it isn't possible?

Recall that you should actively look for ways to reduce risks before they materialize as incidents. Relevant data are essential for making these crucial judgments. The necessary information to facilitate your decision-making process would also be provided by an appropriate risk management procedure.

- **Reduces Individual financial risk**

Risk management courses particularly highlight how important this is for small businesses and sole proprietorships. Your accountability for the debts of your company is directly impacted by the legal form of your company.

Furthermore, in the event of an unexpected business loss or collapse, creditors may be able to seize your assets in order to satisfy their debts if it is improperly organized. By managing your finances, you may protect yourself from such dire circumstances. And regardless of the size of your company, you should generally refrain from guaranteeing any personal debts.

- **Permits pooling of risks**

Sharing risks is made possible through risk management, as in joint ventures. If you don't have the requisite experience, you could choose to try your hand at a new, profitable vertical. Making a single investment in such a venture could get messy.

Therefore, it would be prudent of you to collaborate with a reliable and nimble start-up that possesses the skills and knowledge required to succeed following due diligence through risk management.

Perhaps you could help them with other aspects of their business, like marketing, sales, and advertising while concentrating on developing your core product, as you have a steady and established company. For you both, it is a win-win situation. Additionally, it is a shining illustration of how taking a chance can pay off and sharing expertise.

- **Promotes risk transmission**

Transferring risk from your company to an outside party, such as insurance, is known as risk transfer. There are many different types of business insurance available today to guard your investment and company against damages. You may select the ideal insurance partner for your company by using risk management. Additionally, some insurance companies have policies that can be tailored to your company's needs.

• Converts losses into income relief

In business, one would consciously want to lose money. But losses are inevitable from time to time. With careful financial risk management, you can turn this drawback into a benefit.

For example, careful planning can assist you in converting business losses (either from operations or investments) into tax benefits.

As a result, you avoid paying the standard tax amount. If the losses are connected to capital assets, like stock market and real estate investments, you can even be able to obtain tax reliefs for a number of years.

In a similar vein, effective financial risk management would help you anticipate future drops in revenue and better manage them to obtain associated tax benefits.

- **Facilitates rapid recovery**

Even with complete preparation, there is always a chance that anything can go wrong because of an unanticipated catastrophe. Effective financial risk management can assist you in recovering and avoiding bankruptcy in the event of such a business disaster. If you have a solid risk management strategy in place, you might have money set aside or appropriate insurance to deal with unforeseen business catastrophes and prevent the possibility of a company's failure.

Chapter Seven

The rule of thirds and the concept of portfolio construction

The rule of thirds, which says to "Invest Your Money: One-third in Stocks and bonds; One-third in Real Estate and commodities; One-third in Liquid Assets," is one strategy for accumulating wealth.

A basic guideline for allocating your

funds among several asset classes, including stocks, bonds, real estate, commodities, and liquid assets, is the rule of thirds. To lower risk and boost profits, the aim is to diversify your portfolio among different asset classes. This is how it functions:

Two forms of equity and debt instruments that represent ownership or debt claims on a government or firm are stocks and bonds. Compared to bonds, stocks often offer bigger returns but also higher volatility. Compared to stocks, bonds typically offer reduced volatility along with lesser returns. The risk and return of your portfolio can be balanced by allocating one-third of your funds to equities and bonds.

Two physical asset classes that can see value appreciation over time are real estate and commodities, both of which are influenced by supply and demand. Commodities can generate income through dividends or capital gains from sales, whereas real estate can generate income through rent or capital gains from sales.

You can take advantage of the growth potential of real estate and commodities by allocating one-third of your portfolio to these asset classes.

Two categories of cash equivalents that are readily convertible into cash without significantly losing value are liquid assets. Money market funds,

Treasury bills, certificates of deposit, and bank accounts are examples of liquid assets. Your portfolio can have liquidity thanks to liquid assets in times of need or opportunity. A third of your money should be invested in liquid assets so that you can profit from favorable market conditions or shield your portfolio from unforeseen losses.

To lower total risk and improve your chances of achieving financial success, it is crucial to diversify your portfolio among several asset types.

When it comes to investment, a portfolio is a group of assets that you own or manage, including liquid assets, stocks, bonds, real estate, and commodities. By distributing your funds throughout several asset classes that align with your risk tolerance and financial objectives, a portfolio can help you lower your overall risk and boost your returns.

The act of choosing and allocating assets to build a diverse investment portfolio that satisfies an investor's risk tolerance and financial objectives is known as portfolio creation. The act of choosing and allocating assets to build a diverse investment portfolio that fits your tastes and circumstances is known as portfolio development. Investors can minimize risk and achieve their investment goals with the support of a well-constructed portfolio.

Comprehending the interplay between various asset classes, funds, and weightings, their performance and risk, and how decisions cascade toward an investor's goals is crucial when constructing a portfolio. A variety of securities, including stocks, bonds, and money market instruments, make up the portfolio.

Building a portfolio is a continuous process that needs to be regularly monitored and rebalanced rather than being completed in one sitting. Rebalancing is the process of periodically purchasing or disposing of assets to get one's portfolio back to the intended asset allocation. The process of continuously allocating and redistributing funds among various asset classes within an investment portfolio is referred to as asset allocation.

A number of variables, including the investor's investment goal, time horizon, risk tolerance, market conditions, fund management effectiveness, etc., affect how a portfolio is constructed. You can develop a portfolio using conventional methods or contemporary ones. Conventional methods encompass factor investing, which concentrates on particular attributes of assets like quality, momentum, growth, value, etc. Contemporary methodologies encompass factor-based indexing, which employs astute beta tactics to economically imitate the performance of specific components.

Building a portfolio is a dynamic, intricate process that needs to be carefully planned and carried out. With diversification, it can assist investors in achieving the best possible returns and risk management.

Building a portfolio is crucial because it can assist you in reaching your financial objectives and successfully managing your risk. You can gain the following benefits by doing this:

By distributing your investments over a variety of asset types, including stocks, bonds, real estate, commodities, and liquid assets, portfolio construction can assist you in reducing your risk. By doing this, you can lessen the effect that market swings have on your portfolio and shield yourself from possible losses.

By selecting the ideal combination of assets to fit your time horizon, investment goals, and risk tolerance, portfolio design can help you maximize your returns. This can improve the performance of your portfolio and raise the likelihood that you will eventually receive larger returns.

By offering a logical and consistent framework for making investment decisions, portfolio design can assist you in streamlining your investing process. By doing this, you may avoid making rash or emotional decisions that could hurt your portfolio and save time and effort.

You can review and rebalance your portfolio on a regular basis to keep it at the appropriate risk level and asset allocation with the use of portfolio construction. By doing this, you can make sure that your portfolio stays in line with your objectives and takes into account any modifications to the market or your unique situation.

Conclusion

Many people share the desire to accumulate wealth and achieve financial freedom, but doing so calls for discipline, forethought, and wise decision-making. Setting quantifiable, attainable financial goals that fit your timetable and ideal lifestyle is necessary to accomplish this.

- Create a monthly budget that accounts for all of your out-of-pocket spending and savings, and try your best to stay within it.

- Pay off credit card debt and other high-interest debt, and refrain from taking on new debt unless absolutely essential and advantageous.

- Put money aside for emergencies, major expenditures, and long-term objectives. You should also invest a portion of your income in long-term, diversified assets that will increase your wealth over time.

- Spend less than you make and look for ways to grow your income in order to live below your means

- To prevent unforeseen expenses and safeguard your assets, take care of your health, your possessions, and your insurance requirements.

- If you require direction or advice on how to handle your finances and investments, see a financial counselor.

www.ingramcontent.com/pod-product-compliance
Lightning Source LLC
Chambersburg PA
CBHW050046260726

48658CB00005B/1802